Published by Godzchild Publications
a division of Godzchild, Inc.
22 Halleck St., Newark, NJ 07104
www.godzchildproductions.net

Printed in the United States of America 2016 - First Edition
Cover Design by Maurice Downing of MoDesignz

Library of Congress Cataloging-in-Publications Data
Manifestations of the Kingdom: 30 Days of Reflection
on What God's Reign Means For You/Marc Antoine

ISBN   978-1-942705-32-1 (pbk.)
       978-1-942705-33-8 (ePub)

1. Antoine, Marc. 2. Kingdom 3. Christianity 4. Reflections
5. Devotional 6. Reign 7. Manifestations 8. Spiritual Growth

ACKNOWLEDGEMENTS

Thank you to my parents who taught me through word and deed the importance, the implications, and the standards of the Kingdom. Thank you to the Haitian Diaspora community in Philadelphia, the community which taught me so much about life, resilience, and friendship over the past 25 years. A special thank you to my Fiancée, Chou, who supported me and prayed for me throughout this process.

Most of all, thank you to our Lord and Savior of the world, Jesus Christ! The King who reconciled all of creation back to God and established an everlasting Kingdom that we have already begun to inherit!

DEDICATI✝N

AC5 (My dad, mom, sister, and brother)
Chou, my beautiful Fiancée
The entire Antoine and Cadet Families
HEBC, We All We Got
My Godchildren; Aaliyah, Azalyah, and Noah

TABLE OF
C⚇NTENTS

INTRODUCTION

The Kingdom of God is the authority and reign of Jesus Christ as Lord. It is where the standards of the Creator, the love of Jesus, and the power of the Holy Spirit govern and take precedence. This devotional will help us reflect on what that Kingdom looks like, what the impacts of it are, and how to advance it. This devotional will help align our lives with the Kingdom towards the manifestation of the Kingdom on earth as it is in heaven.

Materials Needed:
1. Bible
2. Devotional
3. Pen/Pencil

How to Read this Devotional:
1. Pray
2. Read the accompanying verses
3. Read the devotional
4. Reflect
5. Pray

PART I
KINGDOM COME FOR US

INTRO
HE IS NOT AFRAID OF YOU!

Luke 7:36-50 NLT

It can be very scary when people who know your past mistakes come around. It can be even scarier when people who know your current sins and struggles come around. Religious people are very good at using your past and your sin to intimidate, exclude, and belittle you. Sometimes they even make you feel as if you are dirty and should not be spoken to or associated with. The Pharisees in Jesus' day were exactly like that! They used the past and the sin of others to marginalize and oppress. They used the mistakes of others to accentuate their own so-called "holiness."

It was no surprise that when the neighborhood prostitute showed up at a dinner that the Pharisees were hosting for Jesus it caused an uproar. The Pharisees were outraged. They thought that Jesus, the supposed sinless prophet, would affirm their contempt for the prostitute's audacity to show up. Not only did she show up, but she proceeded to wrap herself around Jesus, weep all over Him, let her hair down in His presence (which was pretty provocative at that time), and even go as far as to kiss His feet. The Pharisees thought, *surely if Jesus knew what type of life this lady led, He would not let her be at their dinner, and certainly not touching all over him.* But Jesus surprised the Pharisees when he did not react as they expected. Jesus was not afraid of her; her sin did not turn Jesus away!

There are a lot of church folk who may be afraid of your past or judgmental about your present. There are a lot of church folk who may be disturbed by your sin. There are a lot of church folk who would not dare to ever have you over for dinner! SO WHAT?! Be encouraged that the one who forgives sins is not afraid of your past or your present struggles. The one who forgives is always ready

❝ Jesus was not afraid of her; her sin did not turn Jesus away!

to welcome you in. If you have been turned away by the church, embarrassed, and maybe even ignored, take heart in knowing that Jesus is not afraid of your pain, and He will never be afraid of your sin. If you are a church member who sometimes treats others like the Pharisees did the prostitute, don't worry, Jesus is not afraid of that either! Jesus can change your heart! He can help you to see God in your neighbor, even in the "neighborhood prostitute."

No one is past redemption. No one is past forgiveness. Everyone is invited to dinner with Jesus. Do not let anyone make you feel too dirty to approach the table. Love is waiting for you, forgiveness is waiting for you, Jesus is waiting for you at dinner!

EXPECT THE UNEXPECTED
LUCKY DONKEY

John 12:12-19 NLT

E xpectations are powerful! While they can be positive in creating hope for the future, they can also be very dangerous if what is expected does not materialize. On the one hand, expectations, when met, can produce fruits of strength, perseverance, and faith. However, when our expectations are not met, it often results in disappointment, anger, regret, and the fear of future expectations. No wonder the Jews were not so amused when Jesus strolled into town on a donkey.

The Jews were awaiting a messiah that was coming to rescue them from Roman oppression. They were awaiting a social and political revolution. They expected an armed king to ride into Jerusalem on an ornate horse ready to round up the troops and overthrow the empire. They were not expecting a carpenter from Bethlehem to ride in on a lowly donkey preaching a kingdom of peace.

Many of us enter into a relationship with God with a wide range of expectations. We oftentimes end up idolizing our expectations, and when it does not seem that God is working according to our plan, we abandon God and look elsewhere for fulfillment of those expectations. Some of us expect God to bring financial increase, physical healing, professional success, and so on.

While God may very well bless you in all of these areas, do not limit God to just your expectations. God is moving in your life, but it may not be how you expected. Do not miss the move of God by idolizing your expectations. Welcome the donkey and allow the King to do

" Do not miss the move of God by idolizing your expectations.

exceedingly and abundantly more than you could ever ask or think.

SHIFT IN
THE ATMOSPHERE

Luke 1:26-45 NLT

A few years ago, my friend's mother passed away. On the drive to his house, I found myself rehearsing what I wanted to say to him. I drafted a bunch of short phrases that I thought would bring peace and comfort. However, when I arrived at the house, I could not find any words to speak. I sat there with him with my arm around his back listening to him cry. While he was crying, I was trying to find things to say, but nothing seemed right. I felt really bad that I did not have any words of consolation for my friend during his time of grief. After about an hour, he turned to me and said, "thank you." He fell asleep on the couch and a short while after that, I left. While driving home I realized that I did not speak a word the whole time I was there, so why did he say "thank you"? I later realized that sometimes our presence is enough. Being present with him during that time was enough. Sharing in his life at that time was enough. Being close was enough.

Do you know anyone who changes the atmosphere in a room just by their presence? Without speaking or doing anything, do you know someone whose presence alone is enough to change the mood of others? The Bible explains an event that occurred between two pregnant cousins, Mary and Elizabeth. Mary, who was pregnant with Jesus, was going to visit Elizabeth, who was pregnant with John the

Baptist. In Luke's account of the Gospel, scripture says as soon as Elizabeth heard Mary's voice in the house, the baby in Elizabeth's stomach leaped. Mary's voice not only indicated her presence, but also the presence of the baby she was carrying, Jesus Christ.

Jesus did not speak. He did not perform any miracles. He did not preach any sermons that day, but His presence alone changed the atmosphere. The presence of Jesus, even in the womb, brought joy and excitement. Sometimes it feels as if God is silent in our lives. We go through difficult times and need God to speak to us. I urge you to remember that there is power in God's presence. Be at peace knowing that God is with you, even if God seems to be quiet.

What does your presence say about you? When you walk into a room, does it improve the atmosphere? Is your presence a blessing? The presence of God assures me that I am never alone. It

❝ sometimes my presence is enough to shift the atmosphere.

also encourages me that I do not need the right words, sometimes my presence is enough to shift the atmosphere.

BARABBAS
BROTHER OF JESUS

Mark 15:1-15 NLT

Many years ago there was a man living with his twin brother in a small village. The man was very kind, respectful to all, and was never in much trouble. His twin, however, was very rebellious and a big troublemaker. One night, his twin was involved in a fight, which resulted in the death of another young man. One witness saw what happened and in the morning, the police came to the house where the twins lived. The police said they would have to arrest both if neither of them confessed to the crime. The man was aware that his twin had previous offenses and would most likely be condemned to death so instead of allowing his brother to be taken, he confessed to the crime himself. Though he was innocent, he was willing to take the punishment that his brother deserved.

"GIVE US BARABBAS! CRUCIFY JESUS" I wonder what Barabbas was thinking when he heard those words. After being convicted of political rebellion, theft, and violence, Barabbas was sure he would be killed by crucifixion. To his surprise, the crowds were demanding he be freed! Barabbas was guilty; Jesus was innocent. Barabbas was supposed to be crucified on that cross, but Jesus took his place. Just like the twin brother in the previous story, Barabbas did not receive what he deserved, but rather Barabbas's brother came to the rescue.

The name Barabbas means "son of the father." Bar = Son, Abba = Father. Barabbas was a wanted criminal, but none of the crimes he committed ever changed who he was. No problem that he ever created changed who he was. No charge that they pinned against him changed who he was. He was a son of the father. He was a child of God, and because of that, he was a brother of Jesus. Jesus took the cross of a child of God, the cross of one of His siblings. Jesus is Barabbas' older brother (not biologically, but supernaturally) and Jesus is your older brother as well.

No matter what you have done, it won't change who you are. No sin, no problem, no failure, and no insecurity will ever change who you are. You are a child of God and a sibling of Jesus Christ. You are made in the image of God, so in a sense, Jesus is your twin! We are all Barabbas, which means we have all received what we did not deserve... life and another chance!

THE GREAT
TRADE

John 4:1-15 NLT

When Europe voyaged to Africa in the 1400's, they brought with them alcohol and cigarettes. They used the alcohol and cigarettes to trade with the Africans who in turn gave them diamonds and other precious stones. Alcohol and cigarettes in return for diamonds and precious stones... great for Europe, horrible for Africa. Usually, the one initiating the trade is the one who is most in need and has the most to gain. This was the case for the Europeans when they came to Africa, but it was not the case for Jesus when He met the woman at the well.

Jesus is parched from traveling with the disciples and needs some water to quench his thirst. After arriving in Samaria and speaking to a woman at the local well, Jesus realizes that she is just like Him, thirsty. This story is about a proposition from Jesus to the woman. It's a trade for water. The woman gets water from the local well, which her faith tradition places heavy emphasis on as a sacred place. The well is where they get their water for their daily living, but it also represents their culture, faith, and history as a people. Jesus lets the woman know that the well which she so highly reveres, contains water that is temporary. The heritage that the well and the water represent for the woman and her people will never satisfy her and will eventually run out. Instead, Jesus says that she should trade with Him; Jesus will take her water from her well to quench His thirst (physical), and in return, Jesus will give her living water from His well to quench her thirst (spiritual).

What is your source of joy and peace? Where do you go when you are tired and in need? What do you seek to satisfy you? Jesus taught the woman at the well that the thing she gave so much value to, was the very thing that kept her dissatisfied. Jesus is offering us some of His own water, His own life. Jesus proposed to give permanent satisfaction in exchange for her perpetual dissatisfaction. Jesus has not offered you a bad deal; He is not offering you cigarettes for diamonds. Jesus has offered us the greatest deal of all, He has offered us part of Himself. Jesus came to take away the source of our dissatisfaction and to give us living water that never dries out and always satisfies.

JOHN
3:17

John 3:16-21   NLT

The first verse that I ever learned was John 3:16, and like most young people it became my go-to verse whenever I was asked to recite a scripture. The words in that sixteenth verse gave a succinct resume of the gospel message and is arguably one of the most powerful verses in the Bible. John 3:17 is also very powerful but can be overlooked because of the spotlight that is put on the previous verse. Verse 17 gives us a glimpse into the coming of the Kingdom.

WHY:

You do not have to study theology to see that there is something wrong with our world. Poverty, corruption, wars, natural disasters, and so many other indicators point to a broken world. All of these are a result of a fractured relationship with God, a result of sin. The Kingdom came, and continues to come for us in order to restore our full relationship with God. God's purpose is not to destroy or to condemn, God's purpose is to reconcile, to justify, and to save! What would cause God to leave the throne of Heaven in order to rescue a creation that turned their backs on Him in the first place? Well, Love! Verse 16 tells us that God loved the world, and it was this love that motivated God to come to us.

HOW:

When I watch superhero movies I always try and guess how the hero is going to save the people in need. Sometimes the hero has multiple options, which he/she tries before realizing that they don't work. The climax of these stories is usually when the hero finds a wild backup plan and executes it against all odds to save the day. It is a bit different with God. Jesus was always the plan; Jesus is plan

> **" Jesus was always the plan; Jesus is plan A, and there is no plan B.**

A, and there is no plan B. How is God going to save the world? The answer is Jesus. How is God going to restore the relationship of all creation with Himself? The answer is Jesus. How is God going to make all things right that went wrong due to sin? The answer is Jesus! How is God going to save the world from the destruction in which it's headed? The answer is Jesus! Jesus is the way, and the only way. Jesus came to dwell among us and to establish a Kingdom where the will of God would reign! That Kingdom came for us and is still coming…

God's Kingdom came and is coming for all of God's creation, and you are a very important piece of that creation. All of us together make up the world, but our individual value is not lost in the universe. God did not come to judge the world, but rather to save it, and the same is true for you. God did not come to judge you, but rather to save you! While God is responding to the needs of the world, God is also responding intimately to your very personal and specific needs as well. Kingdom, come for us all…

INVITE
INTERRUPTIONS

John 5:1-15 NLT

Verse 6- Jesus: Do you want to get well?
Verse 7- Paralytic: I don't have anyone to help me get into the pool,
every time I try to get in, someone goes ahead of me.

For 38 years, this man lay paralyzed. His only hope of restoration was to get into a pool that was said to have healing power. When Jesus approached him and asked him if he wanted to be healed, he did not even answer the question. Rather, he responded from the context with which he was most familiar. He blamed his circumstances on the lack of help from others. He was used to a lifestyle of lying and waiting. But Jesus interrupted what he was used to and dared him to think differently. Jesus interrupted his life both physically and spiritually. Physically, the paralytic thought his deliverance was contingent upon someone else lifting him up. He had no hope in his own physical capacity. Spiritually, the paralytic thought that his deliverance was contingent upon the moving of the waters when the angel entered; he had no faith in anything outside of the power of the water.

Verse 8- Jesus: Get up! Pick up your mat and walk!

When reading, we usually read verse eight really fast and go right to verse nine where the man is walking. However, we should take our time with verse eight because that is where we find the setup for the come back! The power is not just in the miracle, but in the setup of the miracle. Jesus completely interrupted this man's frame of mind. Jesus interrupted this man's reality. Jesus interrupted this man's normal. Jesus presented to this man an alternative that he never thought was possible.

Sometimes we become so comfortable in a routine and so accustomed to a certain pattern, that we refuse to adopt any alternatives, even if those alternatives prove better than the usual. Sometimes what we are used to becomes what we'd prefer, even if it is destroying instead of helping us. The reason for this is simple, change is scary. Change requires new patterns, new ways of thinking, a new style of living; change requires a deviation from everything normal.

At this point, the paralytic was probably so confused. Should he listen to this random guy who just walked up out of nowhere to introduce an alternative? Or should he ignore this guy and continue with his regularly scheduled programming of lying and waiting by the pool? Jesus made him doubt his physical limitations. After being paralyzed for 38 years, his disability was the norm, but suddenly this random man made him doubt his inability! Jesus also made him doubt his faith. He thought that the waters would bring deliverance, but suddenly, he finds out that believing in the words of this man might bring the deliverance that he needed. The paralytic's life was interrupted with just a few words from Jesus. He was courageous enough to listen to this man. He got up and walked and was delivered of his sickness. He abandoned what he was accustomed to for 38 years and dared to try something new.

What are you holding onto for fear of change? What are you used to that is actually a hindrance and a detriment to your life instead of a benefit and an aid? Jesus shows up and interrupts what we are used to, disrupts the regular and presents an alternative. Do not fear change; embrace it. Do not love the status quo; challenge it. Do not disregard the interruptions; invite them.

JESUS IS NOT
THE "BACK UP" PLAN

Matthew 17:14-20 NLT

In times of trouble, who do you call? Who do you lean on for support? Where does your help come from? Many times, Christians seek out help from trusted family members, friends, pastors, and church leaders; and while it is great to have a dependable Christian village of which we are all a part, we must remember that the village is made up of humans just like us.

I have seen many people become discouraged with their leaders and other people whom they thought would help them but were unable to. I have seen leaders stressed with the burden of giving an answer to solve a problem they didn't really know how to solve. This is exactly what happens in Matthew 17. A man goes to Jesus and complains to him about his disciples and their inability to respond to his need. Imagine running to the person whom you thought could help you, only to realize that they are powerless and cannot provide what you need.

Jesus, we went to your disciples but they were useless. Jesus, we sought after leaders in the community but they did not have the right answers. Jesus, we called on our church family but my son still is not healed!

MARC ANTOINE | MANIFESTATIONS OF THE KINGDOM

BUT WHY DIDN'T YOU COME TO ME FIRST?! WHY DIDN'T YOU COME FIND ME FIRST? WHY DIDN'T YOU CALL OUT TO ME FIRST?

❝ In every situation, Jesus is saying... bring it to me!

Our first reaction most times is to call on everyone else! Turning to God, unfortunately for many people, is an afterthought. After we spend hours talking to someone else, then we think about talking to God. After we spend hours searching the internet for advice, then we think about searching our Bibles. Jesus is not the back up plan! Jesus is the go-to guy every time. In every situation, go to Jesus first! In every situation, Jesus is saying...bring it to me!

THE BAND

Matthew 9:18-26 NLT

In 1982, the University of California (Cal) and Stanford University played in one of the most iconic football games in sports history. It was an exciting four quarters, but with .4 seconds remaining in the game, Stanford was looking towards sure victory with a 20-19 lead. As Stanford prepared to kick the ball off to Cal, Stanford's marching band also began to prepare for the win. With the gamut of musical instruments, the band began to play and then proceeded to march onto the field in anticipation of celebration. However, the .4 seconds on the clock proved to be enough time for a miracle. Cal received the ball and in extraordinary fashion was able to score a winning touchdown on a kick return as the time on the clock expired. Stanford's marching band was so confident of their imminent victory that Cal's receiver had to run through the marching band in order to get to the end zone for the miraculous winning touchdown. When it looked as if the game was over, it wasn't.

One of my favorite stories in scripture is the story of Jesus, Jairus, and Jairus' sick daughter. Jairus' daughter was sick to the point of death and he knew that his only hope would be to find Jesus. He did find Jesus eventually, and when he did, he explained his dilemma and they made their way to the house where his sick daughter was. When they finally arrived at the house, they heard music and people singing which indicated that the girl had already died and they were preparing for a funeral. Jesus came in and said to the band "GET OUT! The girl is not dead!"

" No band formed against you shall prosper!

Many times we are too quick to call it quits. We give up too easily. We call on the band too fast. Everyone in the house and the neighborhood was sure that Jairus' daughter had passed, but Jesus was on His way to make a way. Do not let the band play in your circumstances. In our lives, it may look like things are dead. It may seem that all hope is gone, and we may be ready to give up. But I urge you to fire the band! Jesus is on his way to make a way! The band represents defeat. Stanford's band represented Cal's defeat, and in the same way, the band in Jairus' house represented the defeat of his daughter. But in both cases the band forgot that there is always time for a miracle! Other people may be ready to celebrate your loss, but like Cal did to Stanford, run through the band and go get your miracle! Other people may be urging you to give up, but like Jairus, kick the band out and go get your miracle! No band formed against you shall prosper!

PART II
KINGDOM COME IN US

INTRO
PLANTING SEEDS

Matthew 13:1-23 NLT

One thing I always noticed while watching my mother work in her garden was the big mess she created prior to planting seeds. Before depositing the seed deep into the dirt, she needed to break the soil, and it was the breaking that created the mess. The entire garden looked ugly due to the big mess that the breaking of the dirt created, but what my Mother knew was that the ugly mess was only temporary.

A lot of times, our lives are like the dirt that is being broken for seeds to be planted. The digging causes pain. It reveals things we tried to hide or may not have even known was there, but the digging is necessary in order for God's seed to be planted deep within us. The deeper the roots are planted, the stronger the roots will be in the ground. The Kingdom is coming inside each and every one of us, and if we allow it to be planted deep inside our hearts and minds, the stronger the effect the Kingdom will have in our personal lives.

We are so used to being broken by the world; disappointments in relationships, decisions we regret, and unmet expectations are examples of the pain we have experienced. This pain often causes us to put up walls because we fear being vulnerable; and we try to avoid the mess as much as possible. But my mother knew that the ugly mess in the dirt would one day transform into a beautiful garden. I know that there are some things inside of us that we would rather forget. I know there are some ugly things in our past and some messy situations that we may currently be in, but God can already see the beautiful garden that is coming. Allow God to plant the seeds of the Kingdom inside of your heart and mind. It may create a mess at first, but rest assured, God will turn your mess into a message!

SHEPHERD
OF THE UNIVERSE

Job 38 NLT
Job 39 NLT
Job 40:1-5 NLT

"Where were you when I created the heavens and the earth? Were you aware that I was watching you as you were forming in your mother's womb? Were you there when I gave the waters its parameters or when I hung the stars in the sky?"

Job lost all his livelihoods, his children died tragically, and the love of his life passed away; in a short period of time Job lost everything that mattered to him. These questions are God's response to Job's frustrations. God was not apathetic to Job's struggles but He wanted to show Job that if He could shepherd the universe, He was also able to shepherd Job in times of difficulty. God understands our heartache. He wants us to be assured that He is walking with us every step of the way. We do not know why God allows certain things to occur, but we are confident that no matter what happens, God is in control of it all. Even when it does not make sense and even when it hurts, remember that God is in the midst.

Many of us are lacking peace in our lives, and the reason for that is because we do not understand what peace is. Peace is not the absence of struggle, trouble, or challenges. Rather, peace is the presence of God, the good shepherd, in the midst of those struggles, troubles, and challenges. Peace is when God walks with you through the dark valleys. Peace is when you fear no evil in the face of the enemy. Peace is when your faith abounds even when the situation seems impossible. Peace is when you have hope though everyone else has lost it. Peace is when love conquers hate. Peace is knowing that you should have gone crazy for what you have been through, but God has kept you in your right mind. That is what God reassured Job with. God knew Job was going through the worst experience of his life, but God reassured Job with an understanding that God never leaves and never forsakes His children. Be at peace, the shepherd of the universe is also shepherding your life.

BEHAVIOR MODIFICATION
VS. NEW CREATURE

Matthew 5:21-48 NLT
John 3:1-7 NLT

God is not calling you to be better; God is calling you to be new. Jesus did not sacrifice His life in order for us to modify our behavior; meaning to do more good, sin less, and follow more rules. No. Jesus sacrificed His life in order for us to receive new life. Jesus is calling us to transformation through being born again into new creatures. In Jesus' legendary Sermon on the Mount, He spends significant time articulating the difference between what the law of Moses taught and what He was introducing with the new law of grace.

" God is not calling you to be better; God is calling you to be new.

In that Sermon, Jesus mentions several laws from the Jewish covenant and explains how they were meant to foster appropriate behavior conducive for a relationship with God. The gospel goes further than just behavior. Jesus explains that He desires a change of heart and mind, and the only way for your heart and mind to change is if you become a new creature. God is not simply calling us to stop killing; God is calling us to see our neighbors in the image of God.

God is not simply calling us to stop fornicating; God is calling us to change the way we think about sex. God is not simply calling us to refrain from revenge; God is calling us to humanize our oppressors by overcoming hate with love. None of what Jesus is calling us to is possible by simply modifying our behaviors. Good behavior does not lead to transformation, however, the transformative work of the Holy Spirit in our hearts and minds will result in a lifestyle that is pleasing to God and that manifests the Kingdom. We often think that external changes lead to internal conversion, but the Gospel of Jesus Christ illustrates that authentic conversion is always from the inside-out.

Many of us believe that we have made the Lord proud by clubbing less, smoking less, lying less, stealing less, fighting less, etc. In earnest, God is not looking for moderate sinners, God is looking for radically transformed born again believers. Modified behavior will never allow us to experience freedom in Jesus Christ, nor is it proof of transformation. The lifestyle that testifies to the sovereignty of the Creator, that testifies to the redemptive work of Jesus Christ the Son, and that testifies to the power and anointing of the Holy Spirit is through the revolutionary shift in heart and mind of the new creature.

❝ In earnest, God is not looking for moderate sinners, God is looking for radically transformed born again believers.

Don't be better, be new!

28

COCOONS

2 Corinthians 5:14-21 NLT

In order for the caterpillar to arrive at the final stage of its life cycle, the butterfly stage, it has to go through a season of transformation. This season of transformation occurs within the confines of a cocoon. In human life as well, there is a season of transformation that we must go through in order to start life as a new creature in Jesus Christ. If we pay close attention to caterpillars, we can learn a few things about this important season.

1. The Separation

A cocoon does not have space for two caterpillars. (That right there is a message, go back and read that first sentence again!) Each caterpillar creates a cocoon that is tailor-made for that caterpillar alone. It cannot be joined by another caterpillar or anything else. While separation in our lives may be a scary thought, it is an important process. Many times we are held back from becoming who we are meant to be because we are afraid to spend time alone. Time alone to work on ourselves, to learn, and to mature is never time that is wasted. The transformation of the caterpillar occurs in solitude and the transformation of our hearts and mind must follow suit. We are bombarded by so much noise, so many distractions, and a variety of "stuff"...it is important to create a cocoon that is tailor-made just for you. While separation may be a scary thought, remember that there is a blessing in isolation. The caterpillar remains a caterpillar until it retreats into isolation. Maybe the reason you are stuck in the same season is because you have not retreated into your cocoon yet.

" Don't get comfortable in what is only supposed to be a season.

2. The Fight

After the caterpillar has transformed into a butterfly, the last step is to escape from the cocoon. After being in the cocoon for a period of time, the creature may have gotten comfortable in its setting, but in order to live in the fullness of its being, the butterfly has to break out of what has become its comfort zone. Don't get comfortable in what is only supposed to be a season. Get out of your comfort zone and move on to the next phase of your life. The butterfly breaks out of the cocoon and the world no longer sees a caterpillar crawling on the ground, it now sees a beautiful creature flying through the skies. In order to fly, you need to break out! Fight to fly!

STICK AND STONES MAY BREAK MY BONES
BUT WORDS CAN DO MUCH WORSE!

Genesis 1:26-27 NLT
Proverbs 18:21 NLT
James 3:3-8 NLT

The funny thing about self-esteem is that we treat it as if it has more to do with how others think about us rather than how we think about ourselves. Unfortunately, we base our worth and value on how others perceive us. The reason we do that is because we ascribe more value to what people think and what they say than what God thinks and what God says.

When others say you are not good enough, smart enough, cute enough, strong enough, when others disqualify you, how do you respond? The common response is to visibly disregard their comment and push it off as false, however, if we are honest, we often go away believing what they said. Words have power, enough power to reshape how we think about ourselves. There is a saying that is taught to young children in order to help them deal with bullying, "sticks and stones may break my bones, but words will never hurt me." It's a great tool for kids to use as they deal with the words of their peers during their formative years, but as we grow up we learn with certainty that this saying is a flat out lie. Words do hurt. And often times, words can be more dangerous than broken bones.

Our hope lies in the fact that words are indeed powerful. That is to say, they do not only have the power to hurt but they also have the power to heal. God has spoken words into our lives that have the power to heal and to deliver. Instead of allowing the hurtful words of others to shape your self-esteem and self-worth, allow the words of God to reorient how you see yourself. God said, "let us make humanity in our image!" That is one of the most powerful statements in all of scripture. We are made in the image of God. There is nothing bad, stupid, ugly, or weak about the image of God. The image of God is beautiful in every way. It is perfect, and it is that very image that you resemble. Live with the assurance that God made you especially in His own image. Allow those words to heal the hurt you've experienced from the negative words of naysayers. Allow the words of God to bind you in the truth of God's love. Allow yourself to see yourself in the image of God.

WHEN JESUS
SAYS NO...

Proverbs 3:5-8 NLT

Everyone knows the popular song and saying "When Jesus says yes nobody can say no." It's a great song and definitely a true statement, but what would happen if we turned the statement around? "When Jesus says NO, nobody can say yes"; this statement is just as true but not often as embraced. Here are three important factors to keep in mind as we grow with "no".

1. Accept that No means No

We hate hearing the word "NO" so much that we come up with soothing sayings like, God's no is not a rejection, it's a redirection". When we repeat things like that we lessen God to a genie whose purpose is not to correct but only to grant wishes. When we repeat things like that we dilute God's authority, mock God's wisdom, and ignore His warnings. The truth is that when God says No, God means No. It means that God is literally rejecting that idea, that situation, that route. We should not try to water down God's no or change it into a yes, instead we should accept it. The word "no" is not an appealing word to hear but it is a word that we should get acquainted with and learn to appreciate as God continues to mold and shape us.

2. Rejoice that you know God's will

Nothing is more frustrating than being confused or unsure about a decision. So when God says no to you, rejoice that God has clearly told you what not to do. It's a beautiful thing to know what God does not want. What a privilege it is to know God's will; be glad that God is communicating with you and be encouraged that God is leading you away from trouble.

3. Allow God to be your eyes

God can see farther than we can, and if we allow God to be our eyes, we will keep from falling into unforeseen holes. The bible says that God's word is a lamp unto my feet and a light unto my path. Let God's "No" enlighten your life. When we heed God's word, we manifest light for the journey ahead, but when we disregard the notice of the Lord, we render our eyes blind. Come out of the darkness. Step into the glorious light! Let God see for you, let God be your eyes, and in order to do that you have to let God say "No".

Should we accept sunny days from God but not rainy days as well? God's response will not always be a favorable yes; sometimes it may be a disappointing no. However, God's response, whether a yes or a no, will always be a blessing if you listen.

MIRROR, MIRROR
ON THE WALL

James 1:19-25 NLT

We use mirrors to reveal things about our physical appearance that we would not be able to see alone. For example, the only way to see your teeth is through a reflection. Without it we would never be able to see the teeth inside of our mouths. Our eyes are limited to seeing a certain perspective, but the mirror is a supplement to our eyes, which allows us to see reality from a different perspective.

Just as a mirror reflects our physical nature, the Word of God works as a mirror for our soul. The Word reveals our spiritual nature. A reflection is the imitation or manifestation of an image that is reproduced when light shines on it. So when you open your mouth, light rays bounce off of your teeth, hit the mirror, the rays bounce off of the mirror, and into your eyes. The reflection is the image that is revealed to you by light.

The Word of God acts in the same way as the mirror. Reading the Word is the equivalent of light bouncing off of you, into a mirror, and back into your eyes. The Word of God is the light that reveals your reflection. The Word of God reveals what you look like, and many times it reveals things that you cannot see from your limited perspective. The thing about the Word of God, just like mirrors, is that it tells the truth. It shows you the reality of things. It shows you the true relationship that you have with God. If you had to grade your relationship with God based on your reflection from the Word of God, what grade would you give yourself?

Now that you have graded yourself, what can you do to improve? If you look in the mirror and see crumbs in your teeth, most likely you will stay in the mirror until the crumbs are no longer there. No one goes to the mirror and leaves without correcting what was wrong! There is no point in looking in the mirror if you are not going to improve your appearance. Much is the same with the Word of God; there is no point in reading it if you are not going to make adjustments. Remain in the word of God and continue to work on yourself.

TURN DOWN
THE VOLUME INSIDE

1 Kings 19:9-18 NLT

Sometimes the volume of life is too high! Family, friends, school, work, relationships, bills, responsibilities, ministry, church, and so many other things produce so much noise in our lives. Life often gets so loud that it inhibits our ability to hear the Lord's voice. On the other hand, we don't struggle with talking to God. As children we are taught to pray, sing, and talk as much as possible with the Lord. The church is very good at speaking and making our voices heard, but we are not as good at listening. When was the last time you heard the voice of the Lord? When was the last time God spoke to you?

The story picks up with Elijah waiting on the presence of the Lord to pass by. During the waiting, a big wind blows by and shakes the mountain. After the wind there is an earthquake that trembles the earth. After the earthquake there is a wild fire. The Bible says that the Lord was not present in any of these occurrences; instead, the Lord manifested His presence in a still small voice that Elijah heard after these three wonders. Sometimes we look for God in the wrong places. We look for God in the loud worship. We look for God in the long prayers. We look for God in the fiery preaching... but sometimes God is found in the silence. Can we position ourselves to hear the whisper of God in the midst of life's noise? Elijah was not distracted by the wind; he was not distracted by the earthquake, and he was not distracted by the fire.

Are there any distractions in your life that are keeping you from hearing the whisper of God? Is there anything that is turning your attention away? Turn down the volume of other people. Turn your eyes away from distractions, and stop paying attention to the temptations of the world. Make time for solitude in the presence of God and do not let the whisper pass by without listening.

LOVE
YOURSELF!

Psalms 8 NLT
James 3:13-18 NLT

ormer US President Teddy Roosevelt once said, "Comparison is the thief of joy." While most of us affirm the President's assessment, from time to time, if we keep it real, we still allow ourselves to fall into the trap of comparison. We compare bank accounts, education, relationships, careers, physical appearance and a host of other things, which begs the question, are you happy with who you are? The question is not are you happy with what you have done, or with what you have achieved, but are you happy with the person you are? Honestly, do you love yourself?

Many of us live with an inner struggle that no one else knows about. Most of that struggle is due to the fact that we are not content with who we are. We determine our value based on external variables like the ones above: money, college degrees, marriage, jobs and looks. We measure our worth based on what we can produce and how that production measures up to the standards of society. This type of metric causes us to idolize personal production and external indicators, and for many of us this type of metric leads to self-consciousness and dissatisfaction.

When we compare ourselves to others, we disrespect the beautiful image in which God has made us. When we compare ourselves to others, we are saying that the image in which God has made us is lacking and not good enough. When we compare ourselves to others, we are saying that there is another image that we would rather resemble. Do not let comparison steal your joy. Do not let society dictate how you measure worth. Your worth is not found in anything else but the image in which God has created you.

Our heavenly Father was willing to share His image with you. Jesus was willing to die for you, and the Holy Spirit is willing to live inside of you. Your worth is heavenly. The triune God believes that you are valuable and that is what gives you worth.

ROAD TO
EMMAUS

Luke 24:13-34 NLT

Life's circumstances have a funny way of making us doubt certain things that we were once so sure of. Disappointments and failures often lead to confusion and hesitation, and many times it leaves us questioning what to believe and where to go.

As the two disciples journeyed along the road to Emmaus, they shared their discouragement with a stranger. They explained how they had had high hopes in the man named Jesus. They explained how they thought He was the Messiah and how He was going to lead a revolution to overthrow the Romans and establish the Kingdom of Israel. Finally, they shared how it was three days since this man named Jesus was killed and all they had desired and hoped for was crucified along with Him on the cross.

When God does not come through the way we want and in the time we want, we often begin to doubt and turn our backs in distrust. The Road to Emmaus is a road that we all have been on; it's a road riddled with uncertainty, frustration, and anger. It's a place where we often struggle to keep our faith in God in light of life's circumstances. I had hoped God would move in this way, but He didn't. I had hoped things in my life would begin to change, but they didn't. I had hoped I would be delivered from this situation, but I wasn't. The stranger in the story helped the disciples to remember that our faith should not be based upon God being the kind of God we want Him to be nor should it be contingent upon God's record of granting us our wishes and desires.

❝ No, Jesus did not turn out to be the Messiah that the Jews wanted, but He was and continues to be the Messiah that we need.

No, Jesus did not turn out to be the Messiah that the Jews wanted, but He was and continues to be the Messiah that we need. No, sometimes God does not act according to our wills, but God has and continues to make everything work together for the good of us. Everything works together for our good; the good and the bad, the wins and the losses, the joy and the pain.

The Road to Emmaus is also a road of realization and recalculation. It's a place where what we thought about God comes face to face with the reality of God. It is where we see the manifestation of God in our midst and realize that our lives now will never be the same. The disciples realized that what they thought and what they wanted were nothing compared to what God had in store. They realized that God does keep His promises and recalculated their journey. Jesus was in the midst of those disciples on their journey, and I assure you that Jesus is present on your personal Road to Emmaus. Despite life's conditions, realize that God is present and is keeping His promises. Recalculating…

PART III

KINGDOM COME THROUGH US

JESUS WANTS YOU TO BE GREAT!

John 14:1-14 NLT

Everyone wants to be the greatest. Everyone has visions on how they can make the most impact and be the most influential. As a result, it is rare to find leaders whose dream it is for their successors to be more impactful than they were. Jesus' dream was not only for His disciples to do the same works that He did, but for His disciples to do greater works than He did! Jesus, the Savior of the world, God incarnate, the one who forgives sins, the man who was crucified and then resurrected, yes, that guy wanted His disciples to not only do what He did, but to do more!

There are two things that stand out to me from these words of Jesus.

1.The first is that we need to change our style of leadership. It was William Gladstone who first said "we look forward to a time where the power of love will overcome the love of power. Then the world will know the blessings of peace." Jesus teaches through His leadership style that we should not idolize power, prestige, or accolades. The metric we use for successful leadership should not be based on how many awards we win, but rather on how well equipped and prepared our successors are. Jesus did not love power, but rather, He allowed the power of love to lead His ministry. Jesus was willing to share His power with His disciples because he loved them. Jesus was willing to share His power with His disciples because He did not idolize His authority. Jesus was willing to share His power with His disciples because He realized that the work had to continue after He was gone.

2. Secondly, Jesus has high hopes for us! It's awesome that Jesus has put so much faith in us to accomplish so much for the Kingdom. It is very exciting to know that we are part of God's plan. At the same time, it can be a bit daunting. When I read the Gospels and Acts and hear of all that Jesus did, in the fashion in which He did it, it can become a bit intimidating. What gives me hope is that Jesus has not left us alone. Rather, the Holy Spirit is inside each of us leading and empowering us for the work of the Kingdom. I take heart in knowing that Jesus was speaking with all sincerity when He spoke about our future. God does not call the qualified; God qualifies the called!

Jesus had a dream. It is up to us to fulfill that dream of the manifestation of the Kingdom, on earth as it is in heaven.

LIGHT
BULBS

John 1:1-18 NLT

Light bulbs get all the glory! *Smh.* We often use light bulbs and light interchangeably, but that is a major mistake. The light bulb is not the light! The light bulb is simply the medium, the package, the temple through which the light shines and manifests. Furthermore, in order for the light to shine through the light bulb, the light bulb must be plugged into a power source. Without that connection to the source, the light bulb will never manifest the light. As disciples of Jesus, we are called to be light bulbs. Similar to light bulbs, our purpose is to reflect the light, and the only way to reflect the light, is to remain connected to the source.

The word 'testify' means to reveal, to give evidence as a witness, or to demonstrate. That is exactly what the light bulb does for the light; it reveals the light, it gives evidence to the truth of the light as a witness, and it demonstrates the light's power. How does your life reveal the love of God the Father? How does your life serve as evidence and as a witness to the truth of Jesus Christ? How does your life demonstrate the power of the Holy Spirit?

In a world that gives so much importance to making connections, we must be careful about where and with whom we choose to connect. Do not allow another connection to disconnect you from the source. Once we disconnect from God, there is no light. There is no power. There is no purpose. Make sure your life as Christian testifies about Jesus the same way that a light bulb testifies about light! Check your connections and continue to be a light bulb…the world is in darkness without you!

PUBLIC ENEMY #1

John 12:1-11 NLT

Do you know that your life is a threat to the powers of darkness and your story is detrimental to the work of Satan? Your testimony is a menace to those who oppose the Kingdom of God. For those reasons and much more, you are public enemy #1.

In John 11, Jesus' good friend Lazarus died. Later in the same chapter, Jesus performed a miracle and raised Lazarus from the dead. Lazarus was dead for four days. There was no hope and there was no coming back, but Jesus stepped in and did the impossible. Most of us have never been resurrected from the dead lol, but most of us have stories, examples, and testimonies of how Jesus turned things around for us. Just when we lost all hope, when we thought it was over, when we gave up…Jesus stepped in and turned it!

In the 12th chapter of John, the Bible says that there was a large crowd of Jews who heard that Jesus and Lazarus were in the area. What is interesting is that the crowd was not focused on seeing Jesus, they were focused on seeing Lazarus. Their problem was that Lazarus' testimony was powerful, and it was so powerful that many Jews who heard it started believing in Jesus Christ! Lazarus's testimony was blessing to others, and whenever a testimony is a blessing for people, it's a curse for the enemy. The Jews did not like that this story of Lazarus being raised from the dead was transforming their community, so they planned to kill him.

There is no difference between you and Lazarus. You too have been saved from death to life. You, too, have a story that exemplifies the majesty of God. You, too, have a testimony that can bless and transform communities. Be aware that your testimony is a blessing to those who hear it, and a curse to the enemy. Be aware that you are targeted day and night because your story has power. Be aware that the enemy is out to destroy you because the enemy is threatened by you. However, rest assured that the same God who delivered you is the same God who watches over you. The same God who called you is the same God who will protect you. You are public enemy #1 in the eyes of Satan, but you are a beloved child in the eyes of God!

LEGAL

VS. MORAL

John 8:1-11 NLT

There is a quote that says, "Slavery was legal, the Holocaust was legal, Apartheid was legal, and Segregation was legal. Legality is a matter of power, not justice." In light of that quote, how do we as spirit-filled disciples interact with some of our unjust laws and customs?

Well…what did Jesus do?

The Law of Moses taught that if a man and woman were caught in adultery, they were to be put to death (Lev 20). In John 8, the Pharisees bring to Jesus a woman they caught in adultery with the intention of having Jesus condemn her to death according to the Law of Moses. Since Jesus was a rabbi, they thought he would have no choice but to adhere to the law. "Rabbi, this woman was caught in adultery. The Law of Moses commands us to stone such a woman. What do you say?"

Our faith teaches us that we are to submit to governing authorities, but it also teaches that our allegiance is primarily to Christ, and the morals of the Kingdom of God trumps all laws, policies, and authorities set forth by any governing body. Jesus responded with the famous saying, "let he who is without sin, cast the first stone." This was a radical statement to make; Jesus was making a revolutionary move by establishing His supremacy over the law of Moses.

" As Christians, we need to learn to take some revolutionary positions for the sake of the Kingdom.

As Christians, we need to learn to take some revolutionary positions for the sake of the Kingdom. These positions may not be popular in our culture, they may not be accepted by the masses, and they may even get us in trouble, but these positions are the Christ-like positions. Harriet Tubman, the abolitionist, took a revolutionary stance and took action against the system of slavery in the US. Dietrich Bonhoeffer, the German theologian and author, took a revolutionary stance and spoke against the Nazi Germany regime. Mandela, the political activist, took a revolutionary stance and spoke against the Apartheid system in South Africa. Martin Luther King Jr., the preacher, took a revolutionary stance and led the Civil Rights Movement against segregation in the US. All of these regimes and policies were legal, but none of them were moral. What is going on in your community, society, or country that is unjust? What have you done about it? Jesus is waiting on you to take a revolutionary stance; someone's life is depending on it!

PERSISTENT
IN WAR

Luke 4:1-13 NLT
Ephesians 6:10-18 NLT

We often do not realize the gravity of our decision to be a disciple of Jesus Christ. The Christian life is a war, and nothing less than that. Fortunately, we have been equipped with the proper tools for the war. Ephesians 6 speaks about the armor of God that each and every Christian should put on in order to engage in this lifelong battle. Included in our armor is one offensive weapon at our disposal: the Word of God.

After Jesus gets baptized, He is led into the wilderness and there fasts for forty days and forty nights. The bible says that after the fast, the devil came to tempt Him. In this war, the enemy will tempt us by perverting good things and then appealing to our desires to offer them back to us. In this war, the enemy will attack us by identifying our weakest area, and then taking advantage of it. As the Bible states, "Jesus was hungry", so the devil's first attack was to offer him food. Instead of giving in to the desire for temporary satisfaction, Jesus said no to the devil by using his offensive weapon, the word of God. Jesus used this weapon with all three of the enemy's temptations and was able to overcome each attack. However, the Bible lets us in on an interesting fact. The bible tells us that our enemy is persistent and will persevere in his attacks. At the end of Jesus' temptations, the Bible tells us that the devil left for a while and waited for the next opportunity to return. The devil did not give up after a few refusals from Jesus; instead he waited for another time to come and attack Jesus.

Our enemy does not get tired. Our enemy does not get discouraged. Our enemy is always watching for those whom he can devour. For these reasons we cannot afford to be part-time Christians. We cannot afford to be sloppy soldiers. We must always be on guard and ready to fight. Are you a good soldier? The enemy is waiting for the next opportunity to attack, he will come back, and when he does return, what kind of soldier will he find? In order to fight back, we have to be persistent with the reading and repetition of the Word of God. The scriptures contain the ammunition we need to fire back. Do not neglect your weapon. Master it, use it, and watch as it brings forth victory to your camp.

PRAYER
POWER

Acts 12:1-19 NLT

"But the church prayed."

How often do you pray for people other than yourself? Do you pray for your parents, siblings, aunts, uncles, cousins, and grandparents? Do you pray for your children, nieces, nephews, and other extended family members? How about your friends? Do you pray for them? Do you pray for co-workers, neighbors, strangers, or leaders? One of the greatest ways for the Kingdom of God to manifest through us is by prayer. Church people love to say that we believe in the power of prayer, but our lives sometimes fail to reflect what our mouths profess.

I had a cousin who was constantly getting into trouble. He could not hold a job, he had repeated run-ins with the law, and it seemed as if there would never be any hope for his life. Our family spoke about how we wished he would listen, learn from his mistakes, do better; we also spoke to him repeatedly about his behaviors and what he should do to change his life. One day after a talk with him, I realized that I was always speaking to other people about him, but I never spoke to God about him. I was always telling him to come to church and to pray, but I never prayed for him. I told him that God would listen to him if he spoke to God, but for some reason I ignored the fact that God listens to me too and that I could intercede on his behalf.

" How many of our family, friends, leaders, neighbors, and strangers could be delivered if we only prayed? How many people could be delivered, how many of the sick could be healed, and how many dead situations could come to life again if only we prayed?

In the book of Acts, the bible illustrates the power that the early church manifested through prayer. Peter was put into prison and Herod's plan was to kill him, but the church interceded. The church prayed and God responded by sending an angel to deliver Peter. How many of our family, friends, leaders, neighbors, and strangers could be delivered if we only prayed? How many people could be delivered, how many of the sick could be healed, and how many dead situations could come to life again if only we prayed? Lets take an example from our ancestors in the early church... lets pray.

I challenge you to make a list of 5 people comprised of family, friends, and strangers/groups of oppressed people. Choose a number of days, weeks, or months and pray for them daily. The prayers of the early church were powerful to break chains and set people free. I believe that our prayers can do the same.

IS GOD
SERIOUS?

Romans 12:9-21 NLT

The Bible says that we are to love our enemies, but was God serious about that? The Bible teaches us to bless those who persecute us, but was God intending for us to take that literally? The bible also instructs us that if our enemies are hungry, thirsty, or in need, we should be the ones to respond to their necessity, but did God really mean that? Is God serious? Is it possible to love the person who hates and mistreats you? Is it realistic to live at peace with everyone?

❝❝ We often fail to realize that God does not set standards according to our ability to uphold them, but rather according to God's nature of holiness.

We often fail to realize that God does not set standards according to our ability to uphold them, but rather according to God's nature of holiness. God does not dilute His commands in order to make them more attainable or palatable for us. The standards of God are undoubtedly unreachable for any man or woman, however, God has empowered us through the Holy Spirit to live accordingly. God lives inside of us, and it is because of the indwelling presence of God's spirit that we are able to love our enemies, bless those who persecute us, and respond to the needs of those who hate us. We need to remember that where God leads us, God will also provide. If God is leading us to live a life according to the teaching in Romans 12, God will surely provide the strength, grace, and favor towards the fulfillment of that life.

" You have supernatural strength for the supernatural standards that you are called to live by.

The answer is yes. God really did mean what He said. God teaches us to love our enemies, and God is serious about that. God teaches us to bless those who persecute us, and God is serious about that. If our enemies are hungry, thirsty, or in need, it is the Christian responsibility to respond to their necessity, and God is serious about that as well. Do not focus on your strength, but focus on the strength of God that has been deposited inside of you. You have supernatural strength for the supernatural standards that you are called to live by.

SORRY DOES NOT
CUT IT

2 Corinthians 7:5-12 NLT

The word "repent" is one of those words that is often overused and almost always misunderstood. It is regularly preached on Sunday mornings but rarely applied in daily life. Contrary to popular belief, repent does not mean to confess your sins and ask for forgiveness. Repent means to change your attitudes, your behaviors, and your lifestyle. Repent means to re-route your journey, to turn around, and to walk a different path. Many have confessed their sins and asked for forgiveness, but not as many have repented.

Repentance is a process. It does not automatically happen when you say amen after a long tear-filled prayer. Repentance is a journey of transformation, which requires a complete change-in-direction, a 180.

The 7 step process is laid out in 2 Corinthians 7:10-12. These verses describe what the Holy Spirit produces in a Christian when he/she decides to turn away from sin, to repent.

1. Earnestness - The Holy Spirit deeply convicts the heart and mind of the Christian on the gravity of the sin, and this conviction leads to a serious commitment, intention, and effort to no longer be entangled by that sin. The Christian takes every precaution, step, and careful thought to fight that sin.

2. Clearing of yourself - The Holy Spirit produces a desire of the Christian to become clean. No longer does the Christian want to be identified with this sin. No longer does the person want to be engaged in something that breaks the Lord's heart, and even if the temptation is strong and there is a part of you that craves what is contrary to God, you would rather struggle and starve that desire than to be caught in it.

3. Indignation - The Holy Spirit produces anger and disgust towards the sin. Indignation is an overwhelming emotion in response to what the sin has caused in the life of the Christian.

4. Alarm - a sense of fear and dread rises up in the Christian. This dread and fear is due to the results of the sin, namely separation from God. The Holy Spirit is God, and where sin rules God is not welcomed. When the Christian repents, he/she fears continued separation from the Holy Spirit. It is the desire to remain in covenant relationship with God rather than losing that relationship which motivates the Christian to turn away, to repent.

5. Reconciliation (longing to see me) - Apostle Paul wrote a letter to the church in Macedonia criticizing them for tolerating sin in the church. Paul says that he knows there were people who were mad at him for the stern letter, but it was necessary and it proved to be successful. Often, when people point out our sin, it causes tension, trouble, and drama. However, when a person repents, he/she understands the need for correction from brothers and sisters in the faith. Sin not only creates a vertical gap between humanity and God, but it creates a horizontal gap between humanity with one another. As a result, repentance bridges the vertical gap between humanity and God. It also bridges the horizontal gap between us all.

6. *Zeal* - enthusiasm, energy, and passion. The Holy Spirit produces this kind of fervor in the heart of the repentant Christian for the new direction and the new way that he/she is undertaking. No longer are you devoted to the sin, but you are now on fire for a new way of life. In short, you are on fire for holiness.

7. *Revenge (readiness to punish wrong)* - after living so long in sin and experiencing its impacts, the Holy Spirit produces a sense of revenge in the hearts and minds of those who repent. Not revenge in the sense of repaying evil with evil, but rather revenge in the sense of reclaiming what is yours. The person is ready to punish wrongdoing by saying NO to sin and submitting to God, and by doing that you take back your peace, your joy, and your life.

The best apology is a change in behavior. Saying sorry after every fault is useless if you do not make a decision to change your actions. Repent! Change your thoughts, change your actions, and change your lifestyle. Sorry doesn't cut it.

IDENTIFYING
MARS HILL

Acts 17:16-34 NLT

We spend a lot of time in the church, too much time! I know this statement may be a shocking statement for some, but if we look at the examples through scripture, we are not given a 24/7 model for church attendance. The early church was not content with only having Sunday morning services, periodic revivals and conferences, and weekly church meetings. The early church was undoubtedly dedicated to church life but was also dedicated to its responsibility in the community. The early church was committed to preaching the Gospel outside of the four walls. The early church was happy to sit down, discuss, and reason with others of differing faiths, and Paul exemplifies this during his sermon on Mars Hill in Athens.

When Paul arrived in Athens, he visited the synagogues to speak to the Jews but he also went into the cities and towns to speak with the Gentiles. Greece was full of religious idolaters, pagan philosophers, and spiritual seekers. For many of us, it is intimidating to speak about Jesus to people of other faiths. It is a challenge to present the Gospel to people who stand in strong opposition to what we believe, but Paul gave us a great example at Mars Hill.

All of us have a place like Mars Hill on our journey. Mars Hill is the place where people not only oppose our faith but believe we are delusional for believing it. Mars Hill is the place where you will not only have to challenge the existing culture but also be prepared to be criticized by those who subscribe to that culture. Mars Hill is the place where you will not only have to be creative in your method of evangelization, but also open to discussing and reasoning. Paul used what they knew, Paul met them where they were, and Paul was able to relate. Maybe your Mars Hill is down the block from your house. Maybe it's across town. Maybe it's at school or at work. Wherever it is, speak up and reach people where they are.

Get out of the four walls! Mars Hill is waiting for you.

I PLEDGE ALLEGIANCE
TO THE KINGDOM...

Acts 17: 1-9 NLT

To pledge allegiance to something is to publically declare primary commitment, devotion, and loyalty. It is an oath by which one affirms his/her promise of fidelity. In the book of Acts the Jews are seeking Paul, Silas, and other Christians because they rejected Caesar and pledged allegiance to Jesus, and by doing so committed treason against the Roman Empire.

Our allegiance, loyalty, and relationship with God may make our family and friends feel as if we have committed treason and turned our backs on them. This is what the Jews felt about Paul and Silas, which led them to try and kill the new Christians. When they could not find Paul and Silas, they went to Jason's house, another disciple, and dragged him into the streets. They demanded that Jason and the other Christians leave the city because they were causing a disturbance.

Your allegiance to the Kingdom can get you in trouble, but it's better to be in trouble with the world and safe with God, than to be safe with the world and in trouble with God. To deny the powers of this world is to disturb it. Do not be afraid to disturb the empires of darkness. Do not be afraid to turn the world upside, and do not be afraid to be persecuted for truth because the King to whom you pledge allegiance has also pledged allegiance to you! When God became man, He pledged His allegiance to you. When Jesus took your guilt, shame, and sin on the cross, He pledged allegiance to you. When Jesus resurrected on the third day and declared victory over death, He pledged allegiance to you. When the Holy Spirit entered you, sealed you for the day of redemption, and began to transform and conform you to the image of Christ, he pledged allegiance to you. God has pledged allegiance to us over and over again!

" Do not be afraid to turn the world upside, and do not be afraid to be persecuted for truth because the King to whom you pledge allegiance has also pledged allegiance to you!

What takes precedence in your life? Is your ethnicity your priority, maybe your last name, your city/country, your college, or your church/denomination? What or who do you pledge allegiance to? I encourage you to think again, reflect on your priorities, and review where your loyalties are. Pledge allegiance to the Kingdom of God. In the face of temptations pledge allegiance to the Kingdom. In the face of struggles and disappointments, pledge allegiance to the Kingdom. In the face of life's challenges, pledge allegiance to the Kingdom. Let us continue to be a disturbance in this world towards the manifestation of the Kingdom!

www.ingramcontent.com/pod-product-compliance
Lightning Source LLC
Chambersburg PA
CBHW060144050426
42448CB00010B/2284